NURTURING VS. DAMAGING CULTURE

Unleash the Full Potential in Your Organization

Fred MOUAWAD
Illustrated by Julien BORDEAUX

Nurturing vs. Damaging Culture
Fred Mouawad
Illustrated by Julien Bordeaux
Edited by Kevin J. Rosser
Layout by Sarintorn Chanitrapirak

NURTURING VS. DAMAGING CULTURE

Unleash the Full Potential in Your Organization

Organizations are formed of people who interact with each other and with external parties following explicit and implicit guidelines that form a company's culture. Culture is thus the mental map that guides the actions and behaviors of the people within the organization. From our experience, culture in an organization can either be a great asset or a liability. It can either nurture relationships and increase connections and performance of teams by coordinating efforts toward common goals, or it can do the opposite and damage relationships, sending execution into disarray and waste resources that ultimately destroy value. This illustrated book is meant to contrast what we believe are good nurturing behaviors—those that will nourish relationships—with those that we think are damaging—behaviors that limit the development of the organization and often destroy the very foundation of what an organization is trying to achieve.

We encourage all readers to think of their own work environment, identify behaviors they think are nurturing vs. damaging, and then figure how as a group these behaviors can be made more explicit and help those that are, at times on the damaging side, move to the nurturing one.

Our basic belief for building a high performance organization is to make sure that all positions are filled with people who have the right skills, the ability to grow, and are highly motivated to drive continuous improvements in line with the vision of the organization. To achieve these goals, leaders at all levels are responsible for defining the culture that will drive the expected behavior of their team members. Putting your organization into a nurturing mode will unleash its true potential.

Fred MOUAWAD

NURTURING VS. DAMAGING CULTURE

Unleash the Full Potential in Your Organization

PREFACE

Damaging Culture

Little input is taken from people in lower ranks, and there is a disconnect between orders coming from above and what is required on the front line.

Look people, it's my way or the highway!

■ *"I am the manager and I know much more than my subordinates. I should tell them what to do and they should execute without questioning my authority."*

Nurturing Culture

Get as much information from a variety of sources to study the issues and options available. Invite input and work collaboratively with all parties to make informed decisions in the interest of the organization.

■ *"My role is to empower my team to search for the best possible solutions, and have them make their recommendations to me backed by data and facts."*

Damaging Culture

People earn their salaries and feel disconnected to other departments and the overall success of the company. They work just to earn their monthly pay.

■ *"Let me do the strict minimum to earn my salary at the end of the month. Anything extra is not worth it."*

Nurturing Culture

People find meaning in what they do and understand how it relates to the overall strategy of the company. They feel a sense of partnership and are motivated to see the company succeed and therefore will stretch to work and collaborate with others to win as one group.

■ *"I want to be part of a group that wins and I therefore will give my best shot at everything I do to move the organization forward."*

Damaging Culture

Hide problems to avoid getting
in trouble and being blamed for them.
"Shooting the messenger."

Why is he so angry? I am not the one who made the mistake, I am just reporting it.

■ *"I'm not going to be the one to speak up when problems or issues arise. Let me just focus on my own work and not do any more than asked. That way, I stay out of trouble."*

Nurturing Culture

It is the responsibility of all people in the organization to identify opportunities for improvement and raise red flags. Those that do are appreciated for their initiative. Opportunities are welcome so we can continuously improve.

■ *"If I see something wrong I am happy raising a red flag knowing that my manager and my colleagues will appreciate the opportunity to improve."*

Damaging Culture

Find a scapegoat to blame and punish so others will be afraid to make the same mistake.

■ *"Punishment is the ultimate way to teach and to impose my authority."*

Nurturing Culture

Take quick corrective action to remedy problems. Then investigate to find the root causes, and think of how the problems can be prevented in the future by improving the Company's management system.

■ *"Addressing the root cause and figuring how not to repeat the same mistake in the future are my key priorities."*

Damaging Culture

Not to share knowledge for fear of being replaced.

Better be safe than share.

"I'm afraid if I teach someone to do my job they will fire me and put someone else in my place that earns less."

Nurturing Culture

The more knowledge we share the more problems we can solve as a group and the more valuable we become to the company. A great fisherman who can teach others to fish is more valuable than 10 great fisherman who can't teach.

■ *"Teaching allows me to grow and it increases my value towards the organization."*

Damaging Culture

Without threats and coercion, no action is taken.

I am not taking action until I'm told to!

■ *"The least I do the less trouble I get into. Why take any chances."*

Nurturing Culture

People are self-driven and focused on continuous improvements so they identify opportunities, plan well, and relentlessly focus on execution to create value.

■ *"I have a strong desire to improve the world around me while understanding my key priorities to advance the organization."*

Damaging Culture

Day to day work to solve current problems and crises. "Fighting fires."

■ *"I am facing too many daily challenges so I can't plan or do more than my routine work."*

Nurturing Culture

Plan for the future and anticipate problems.
"Fire prevention."

■ *"I have a good sense of what I want to accomplish today, this week, next month and this year. I also have a vision for the next three to five years and I am organized to get all projects done on time."*

Damaging Culture

Avoid making hard decisions so we are not later blamed if something goes wrong.

■ *"Why should I make a decision if it will bite me back in the end?"*

Nurturing Culture

Team members are always thinking about how the organization should be making smart decisions to create the most value. They raise their concerns when they sense the company is not going in the right direction and share their ideas on how to further improve.

■ *"Good decisions across the board are of benefit to the entire organization."*

Damaging Culture

Favor certain groups of people based on subjective criteria such as beliefs, compliance, nationality, and/or religion and treat that group differently from the rest. "Us" vs. "them" mentality.

■ *"I just don't trust people that are not similar to me."*

Nurturing Culture

Every single person is respected for who they are and how they work regardless of nationality, age, ethnicity, or religion. We believe in a meritocratic system. Everyone is given a chance to perform.

■ *"I don't judge people superficially. I spend time learning about how special each person is and how they can contribute positively to the company."*

Damaging Culture

If people don't perform, reprimand them frequently.

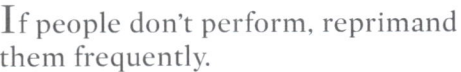

No, no, no! That's not it again. How many times do I have to tell you?

■ *"They just don't get it! I have to keep shouting and pressing them to perform."*

Nurturing Culture

Bring members on board that are proactive and want to learn, and give them regular feedback. Redeploy within the organization or free team members that don't meet expectations and are not progressing. You are only as good as your team members.

■ *"The right people in the right positions focused on the right projects and working well together is how we are going to drive high performance. I can't afford to keep laggards on my team."*

Damaging Culture

Getting angry when a mistake happens is the expected norm.

■ *"The more I show my anger, the more I assert my authority, and the more others will fear me."*

Nurturing Culture

I control my emotions in order to investigate the situation fully so I can take the most appropriate action.

■ *"By staying cool headed, I can think best through the situation I am facing, so I can take the right steps and be perceived as fair by all involved."*

Damaging Culture

People fight for survival and if someone does not respect them they will do whatever they can to work against them so they fail.

■ *"You stab me openly and I will stab you in the back."*

Nurturing Culture

Respect is at the core of team building and working collaboratively. Respect is earned so each team member remains highly sensitive to how they interact with others. They avoid pointing fingers and always refer to facts and processes to avoid blame.

■ *"I treat all people with respect and dignity. I generally treat people the way I would want to be treated."*

Damaging Culture

Damaging or destroying company property or materials through misuse or negligence causing increased operating costs. Over consuming and ignoring wastage as it does not have a personal impact.

■ *"Why should I worry about preventive maintenance? If the printer breaks down, the company will pay for it. Not my problem."*

Nurturing Culture

Be sparing, thrifty and economical with respect to all company assets whether property, materials or stock as if they were your own. And always use and consume in a conservative and moderate way to avoid wastage and damage.

■ *"Any asset that does not add value is removed from the work place. I have around me only what I use, and I keep everything in good condition, clean, and in the right place."*

FRED MOUAWAD is a serial and portfolio entrepreneur and founder of Synergia One Group of Companies (www.synergiaone.com). Synergia One is the entity that groups all the companies he founded and includes the family jewelry business, Mouawad, of which he is the fourth generation.

Fred grew up in Geneva, Switzerland, where he attended boarding school at College du Leman. He received his Bachelor of Science in Business Administration from Pepperdine University, where he was also a teacher's assistant for the Business Policy & Strategy course. He is a Graduate Gemologist from the Gemological Institute of America, and has co-authored articles in the field of gemology. He is an alumnus of the Harvard Business School (MBA) and of the Stanford Executive Program (SEP) at the Stanford Graduate School of Business. Fred is trained in Lean Six Sigma and ISO 9001. He is also a member of the Young Presidents' Organization (YPO).

**Wishing you
nurturing success!**